MYSTERY
Within

This book is dedicated to all the Children
of the world. Past, present and future.

A special dedication to Phoenix, Lucy,
Abraham, Meseret, Bella and Adam who
have appeared in the Mystery Within.

Balboa Press books may be ordered through booksellers or by contacting:

Balboa Press
A Division of Hay House
1663 Liberty Drive
Bloomington, IN 47403
www.balboapress.com
1 (877) 407-4847

ISBN: 978-1-5043-0574-7 (sc)
ISBN: 978-1-5043-0575-4 (e)

Print information available on the last page.

Balboa Press rev. date: 02/27/2019

BALBOA
PRESS
A DIVISION OF HAY HOUSE

Mystery
Within

JODIE CHILD

Illustrated by: Stephen Adams

Man

Woman

Boy

Girl

We are not our skin

We are not our bones

We are not the pleasures
that allow us crazy tones

We are not the objects
that live in our homes

Stars and moon at night

Sun and rain in the day

Walk with nature and
let it guide your way

Somewhere there you
will find the mystery in
your day and night

Take the courage and
meet your light. For there
you never have to fight

Open your door and see your light. It is waiting for you through the day and night.

You are magnificent
just as you are.

Shine yourself as bright
as a star because........

You are the mystery within.

About the Author

Jodie Child a Children's Yoga and Meditation Instructor who has a passion for Children's wellbeing. For nearly three decades Jodie has engaged as an Early Childhood Educator and worked with Government Agencies for the welfare of young Children.

Jodie loves seeing the true essence of a child shine as brightly as possible!

LET'S BUILD CONNECTION

Hand Appreciation

Our hands are covered in skin

Beautifully formed in their own peculiar way

The beauty they hold when used in a positive way

Filled with lines unique to themselves

Hands are a powerful tool they help us connect in the most incredible way
Textures they feel to guide us through our day
Hands help nurture our bodies in a practical way
So be grateful for your hands and let them bring joy to your day
Give them a kiss for all the help they have given you today

Crystals are a great way to build connection. They are an element of Mother Earth that carries their own unique energy vibration.

Who is ADAM??

Adam has a natural ability to connect and communicate with crystals and stones. He began his spiritual journey at a very young age being able to hear and sense the frequencies of stones from his older sister's rock collection. Soon he was giving rock treatments to family members and friends. At the age of seven, Adam created his first crystal grid.

It happened one day while he was waiting for his mom to finish a project. Adam was bored, so his mother gave him several small Lemurian crystal points and told him to go play. When she came out of her office, she was astounded to find what Adam had created - an amazing, geometrical grid that had an incredible amount of powerful energy running through it.

Adam has been recognized by Spirit Science, Gaiam TV, Doreen Virtue, and Healing Crystals. He now embarks on the next phase of his journey - healing the planet. He has created several World Grids with the help and assistance from people all over the world.

His website is www.crystalgridmaker.com
His facebook page: https://www.facebook.com/crystalgridmaker/

Connecting to the Grid
Grid made by Adam

This grid consists of flourite, geodes, rose quartz and tiger's eye. The grid is supposed to help and heal all people the book mentions and all people who read the book. Some of the healing abilities the grid includes are healing of mind, body and spirit. Anyone who wants to use this grid has to set their own good intention and has to believe in the grid and their own ability to heal and to love.

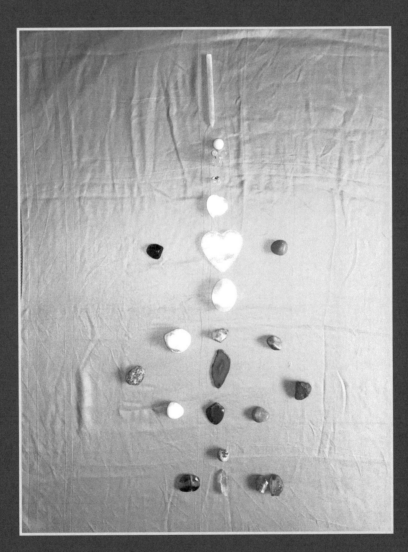

Another important factor is to connect to the crystal heart in the middle of the grid to symbolize love and hope. If you want the healing of the grid, then you have to accept the healing. The angels symbolize trust and compassion. All of the crystals work together to create the calm, healing feeling.

Mother Earth

Breathe her air in deeply

Swim and have fun in her water

Feel the warmth of her sun on your body

And dance like a burning wavy fire

Walk gently and softly on her

And lay down on her and feel the vibration of her love

Dedication to the Butchulla People

Fraser Island - Hervey Bay

Queensland Australia

Totem the Yul'lu Dolphin

Printed in the United States
By Bookmasters